black bird blue

poems by

Broderick Eaton

Finishing Line Press
Georgetown, Kentucky

black bird blue

Copyright © 2022 by Broderick Eaton
ISBN 978-1-64662-862-9 First Edition
All rights reserved under International and Pan-American Copyright Conventions. No part of this book may be reproduced in any manner whatsoever without written permission from the publisher, except in the case of brief quotations embodied in critical articles and reviews.

ACKNOWLEDGMENTS

"stream" appeared in the November 1, 2017 issue of The Source Weekly as a 3rd place winner in the *Source*/OSU-Cascades MFA annual poetry contest

"when we were mud", "the afterlives of leaves", "blackbird", and "flight" appear in *Sixfold*'s Winter 2019 issue

"black bird blue" received Honorable Mention and came out in the 2019 *Crosswinds Poetry Journal*

"falling stars" won the New Poets category of the *Oregon Poetry* Association's 2019 spring contest and was published in their *Verseweavers* 2020 prize anthology

"bird house" was published in the 2019 issue of *Flying South* magazine

"vespers" received Honorable Mention in the 88th Annual *Writer's Digest* Poetry Contest

"argentum" was 3rd place in the 2019 the *Source*/OSU-Cascades MFA annual poetry contest

"two miracles", "shatter proof", "old crow", and "three mississippi" won first prize in the winter 2020 *Sixfold* Magazine Poetry Contest

"in the shadow of atlas" was published in the 2020 *Crosswinds Poetry Journal*

"the shape of sound" was runner-up for the 2019 Erskine J. Poetry Prize and was published in *Smartish Pace*

"to touch the light" was a finalist for *Bellingham Review*'s 49th Parallel Award

"even as" won 3rd prize in the 2021 The *Source* Weekly/OSU-Cascades MFA annual poetry contest

"communion" and "salmon fly" were selected for the 2021 *Clackamas Literary Journal*

"the one who leave the ground" was published in the 2021 *Crosswinds* Poetry Journal

"crow murder crow" was included in the 2021 *Slippery Elm Literary Journal*

Publisher: Leah Huete de Maines
Editor: Christen Kincaid
Cover Art: Melissa Eaton
Author Photo: Flynn Eaton
Cover Design: Elizabeth Maines McCleavy

Order online: www.finishinglinepress.com
also available on amazon.com

Author inquiries and mail orders:
Finishing Line Press
PO Box 1626
Georgetown, Kentucky 40324
USA

Table of Contents

falling stars 1
clams 2
two miracles 3
to touch the light 4
vespers 5
when we were mud 6
stream 7
september on the deschutes river 8
flight 9
shatter   proof 10
blackbird 12
the afterlives of leaves 13
crow murder crow 14
bird house 15
old crow 17
in the shadow of atlas 18
three mississippi 20
communion 22
the shape of sound 23
salmon fly 24
the memory of glaciers 25
even as 27
the ones who leave the ground 28
argentum 30
black bird blue 31

*To MO, who saw something in me
long before I could see it in myself.
And always, to my Stuart,
for being everything I never knew I needed.*

falling stars

right there in the hidden chambers of your heart
I was born before I was born where your muscles squeezed
with apprehension, where your pulse drummed
its anticipation and you knew me before you knew me

when you called for my light to paint a new trail in your sky
I fell from stars, fell into the arms of a family tree
the same way you fell into yours and yours became mine
we fell from the heavens to roots threaded deep in the soil
of our grandfathers where decay becomes riches and we rise
as trembling sprouts clasped fast to woody anchors

now, the coins of your limbs have spidered and dropped
into rusting twilight and I see the door you will leave through, there
I will stay and the rhythms of my blood will wave goodbye
letters on our shared strands forming the words my mouth cannot

we will remember each other in the way
we best understood, me sleeping on pillow cheek
tiny bubbles at my suckle mouth, you staring at ghosts
in the flashes of an early morning fire, relaxed in the quiet
wilding dreams of your domesticated heart as you untangle
your branches and stir the sparks, warming the house

clams

a small pile
of kelp wrapped
bones too ossified
for fish too slender
for seal or whale
just the scaffolding
of some bird resting
near a disembodied claw
from a right-handed crab
the slick white remnants
picked clean

dad chooses a bone
with a sharp point
uses it to pry a clam
the size of his palm
a young geoduck that tried
to flee on its single
obscenely thick foot
but his shovel so fast
so experienced the clam
never had a chance

the bone now
our fork we eat pieces
of valve and siphon
muscle and gut still pulsing
the slippery flesh torn
from its pearled housing
rinsed in the ocean
as waves pull the sand
from beneath our sinking feet

two miracles

the first, when you arrive
fallen from stars
into the bare mountains
of your story untold
wet and slow to awaken
your wings unfold in deep
and wanderous valleys as you learn
to pick up your shadow, carry it
in the shifting shape of yourself
and roll dust from between your toes
after everlong days of walking
trailing the sun across the sky
falling and rising, falling and rising
gathering seeds in your skin
and bees in your hair as you speed
flower to limb to peak and finally there
you pause, long
enough to quiet the bees, to feel
the earth's iron pull against your bones
hear the wind calling your name
in a language you have forgotten

when you step down from the top
into the known unknown afternoon
amber glow of failing day etches
a view more precious in descent
as footprint following footprint you diminish
teaspoon by teaspoon digging your grave
in mudding light, the sun lands one last time
and you follow lightning bug lanterns
into the darkness, to the other miracle
when you lay yourself down
next to your shadow untethered
free of your rusted frame you answer
the wind in its language remembered
fly back to your constellation
to your waiting cocoon in the stars

to touch the light
—on Mary Oliver's "Fletcher Oak" at Sweet Briar College

see the acorns scattered
full of their own wooden visions
of one day trunks, of thickened roots
run deep and stained
red with clay

feel the live silence
        —no, interpret with your bones
her vibration burrowed into the marrow
of your malleus where it presses the taut
drum inside your ears

in september clusters the acorns
start their fall, their eventual rise
from pale fingers pushed
by fate, by rain breaking through
the rich sponge of ironblood earth

reaching into the light once more
here, her leaves, hear them whisper
your name as they call the drifting sun
the mighty ticking calendar, the fading
crimson god circling our days

marry yourself to this moment
this brief cellulose dream
marry all of her generous growth
arms thrown open to the luminous
let it flow down and down

listen, open your bursting shell

vespers

whisper your vespers to the dying
light as it decomposes
where the last birds flirt
with darkness diving through
a frantic net of gnats snarled
hovering above the lake
twilight pilots, they lithely ply
crepuscular glow filling
their tiny bellies and disappear
wing-tucked into the trees

there, where night has already landed
branches clasp hands overhead
and the empress of summer gathers her riches
leaf-laden and adorned in fat coins
generously spread like a mother hen
beckoning, beckoning you under
you will fall
beneath her deep spell convinced
this moment is always
this prayer will not be your last

from the safety of your blessings pressed
back against bark against trunk
where habit pushes life through cellulose veins
sail your prayers for the good you cling to
the god you sing to is a creator and a thief
your savior paints the green you savor then steals it
away, slows the sap and severs the root
speak your gratitude as you feel the tree
between your fingers and breathe for now
you are divinely, relentlessly alive

when we were mud

stirred from mud   we stood
forgot our filth   the dirt beneath
the crescents of our fingernails   maybe
we departed before the mud dried   maybe
we arrived before we were formed
maybe   we didn't remember
   we were dirty

when we were mud   we knew this
but we rose and forgot
that standing is just the start
of the need to lie down   to tie our eyes
with sutures of sleep   eventually
one by   one
we sink into the furrow of time
feel a change   crease   the first petal
the perfect cup of a tulip collapses
the wheel of each flower spins into dust
every leaf trades green for fire every stone
softens for the river every beat
of your heart is a pump closer to falling
back into the earth

soon   my mud will dry   so
   open the heavens
let the rain fall into pearls   on this skin I wear
wash the dust back to my feet   let
my petals curl out of the way for the next
blossom might mean more   the next
leaf will rust into glorious tatters   the last
beat hammers into stillness
and we remember everything
   everything is borrowed.

stream

there is a process by which
water disappears
when we are not looking
they say it flies
    weightless
through our sky then
falls back to earth
heavy and new

one hot summer afternoon
we followed a mountain stream
to see what boulder birthed it
what stone was responsible for this
    oh, sacred spot
where lusty gush poured
from beneath the earth
as though the planet
were a pitcher tipped
just enough this way
and we were satisfied

miles later
where the water flattens
    quiets
runs wide to fill
an alpine bowl waiting
with hard open hands we slid
bare feet through the cold
savored the late blue release
when earth gives back
heat taken from the day
crickets sing from deep
in meadow grass
when the dusky remains
of light become
ashes to mountain
dust to lake

september on the deschutes river

old crow laughs low
dragging his shadow down the river
where two willows twinned
from the same trunk anchored
deep beneath the riverbank
send serpents of root rising through soil
as they lean across the water
caress the current with green fingers
tinged in orange tasting
the fleeting history of snow
the slow cataclysm of falling
the inevitable pull of ashes and ocean

flight

is there wonder is there light
when time has fled when
the heart trembles its last when
your hand is not there inside your hand
      this was always meant to happen

do you stand balanced between mountains
or are you wrapped inside a cloud or
do you drink the river whole as
you swim like a salmon to completion
      this is the natural order

what sky do you feather with raindrop wing
can you still see the shiver of a lily stem can you
feel the last paint of sunset brush your skin do you
hear the hawk scree as it streams toward the earth
      you need to get over this

will you remember a black so black
it reflects green a song so sweet
you can't possibly think when some tiny miracle
makes you catch your breath
are you still   still

shatter
       proof

because love always ends
that's just the way it works
I was already broken before
my hand ran down her side
pressing river water from her fur
when the cradle between my thumb
and index finger stopped
against a fleshy mass hidden
under the soft double coat of her hip

smaller than a golf ball, maybe
like one of those little limes at the store
at first, I thought it was her bone
popped out of place from jumping
after a rabbit on yesterday's walk
but I knew it wasn't so simple
the fracture that wasn't captured
when I stood back up last time
sent tendrils skating through my chest
pausing my heart
pulling apart what was left
of my smooth surfaces

I remember my father's doctor, his metallic words
each falling like an anvil through my gut
tunneling through the DNA that bound us
terminal
as if he were a bus
aggressive
as though he were a dog
lung
which isn't where it started
as if it could be trained, would stay in place
once identified

then the vet, holding my gaze like a warm hand
this isn't the kind we do anything about
so we waited, not really waiting
but what do you call it
when you see the end that hasn't happened yet
she will eventually encounter pain
which she didn't,   or
it will outgrow her body's ability to accommodate
which it did,   so
we traced the intricate vascular system
it created for itself through paper skin
we watched as it grew and we knew
she would soon chase the same shadow
that swallowed my father
the soft bodies of my grandmothers
and cat after cat after cat
that thought it was faster than cars

blackbird

blackbird bobs on a branch
I think this dance is the wind
but then I see it is his own weight
too great for the slender stem
clutched in the circle of his toes

he peers with intense button eye   just one
as though he has found what he came to visit
behind bright shouts beneath
his dark mutterings I hear
the things he doesn't say   the things
he can't wrap with sound
I don't know the words either
but in the bristled thrust
of crimson epaulets I sense
the urgency I hear the boulder
of his thoughts the fear that maybe
night will come with some pearl unsaid
some idea too big for this song some sigh
that can't be heaved because its weight
would break us would make us
fall from our tree

with one flap he fades into the spilling night
this darkness is a kindness
maybe
the other is too

the afterlives of leaves

(komorebi: tree leaking through sun
the miracle of light, leaves)

cellulose bones strung like ribs parched in the sun
woody webs spread over their own decay
glowing fiber fingertips draw roadmaps to their end
do they remember seizing the light as it fell
driving cupped hands upward in worship?

when you get there will you know
if you are broken into fractals of yourself or
just broke down   waiting   with your back to the light?
will you remember the flavor of the last laughter
as it fell from your lips and you sipped time
from the silty swirl at the bottom of your cup?

look up at the heavens where it all starts over
where we strung our words on the spokes of the stars
for later   always later   they flutter and rustle
as we sift for order and cling to each other hoping
to hold the light before it passes

crow murder crow

(n) crow: clever featherglint so black it's no longer black but instead shines green like want and maybe that's why he covets what shines what reeks   what feels lost to another once it is gone

(n)(v) murder: they show up black tie noisy dressed to kill but did that one crow on the branch above me actually kill the little black cat whose head it dropped to crack on the ground at my feet not three minutes after a man asked me to keep an eye out for his lost black cat   or did the crow overhear and bring the coyote-damp head as an answer to this man's loss so that the hole in his family could fill with a flood that would gradually subside instead of staying empty from not knowing   when I run across the new topography after yesterday's storm where new rivers careened down from the ridge making deep ravines that branch smaller and smaller until they are like a drained vascular system laid on the earth's surface   I think it looks like the dried-out rivulets of the american west that thirst for another storm and I wonder if this is what the world looks like to a crow in search of shiny treasures

(v) crow: shouts and laughter I misinterpreted for too long   maybe sometimes they tell stories to remember the way through the changed landscape   all those new ravines   maybe when someone says earth-shattering they don't really mean the damage to the land itself but to the things they love that drag their small lives across it

bird house

deep
inside a box inside
a notch inside the spine
of a long tilting tree lie
the tender remains of a small nest
the birds who built it
have flown, leaving behind
feather, function, purpose, intent

the window into its reedy center is the same
as the hole right through my heart
that pumps, pumps, squeezes life
and lets it flow   if you put your ear right up next to
this cleft, my heart, you might hear
thump-echo
       thump-echo
              thump—

...this is when memory speaks and we are suspended
together, kindred in the sanctuary of what we knew
revisiting this temple as if it's our religion and
offering recollection as reverence, tithing in tears

thump-echo
the heart flutters back into its chamber
because it must, if I am to stay
pressed faster to catch up to now
       thump-echo
I keep that space open
       thump-echo
for when you return
to this place, your flown ghost resurrected
       thump-echo
long enough to whisper into the box inside
a notch inside the spine of a long tilting tree

and we remember
thump
        echo
we remember

old crow

oldcrow settles wingfold glossed
brushdeath suddensit by my side
bitrust voice airscratches harsh
unsettles my quietmind to answer
the don'tdare question
    I don't dare ask

but oldcrow knows
old soulfetch knows mytime and folkworry
not yet, you, muddletalk crowspeaks
steadies my flutterheart clutchbeats
    but who, then whotime now
thoughtscatter I carefulwatch
the regal shinebeak slowturn
greenglint black feathershimmer
peering eyespy one side
to the other, patientknowing
    patientknowing he waits

beadblack buttoneye lands
where swiftbrown birdswoop
neatly quickends spidercrawl
ohsoclose my startlefeet
    crowtoes bent watches brownbird fly
legsprawled spider to waitbabies nested
their needcries treed nearby

beakspread he laughcaws
    see? evermore you live until you don't
unfurls paperdash wings and jumplifts
airstroke into the evelight
    see you soonlong
he whisperscrapes
        soonlong
into the nextwind of thisnight

in the shadow of atlas

we lie
melting gold with the river
as the aftermath of light dives
into night, seething and then silent
with the earth
sighing beneath our backs

there, in his palm
where the sun buried itself once more
deep in the shadow of atlas' stony grip
knuckled mountains rest unmoved
by change, unchanged
by our repetitions

broken
remainders of time stretch
without meaning, without measure
lost with the peaks in the darkness
reminders that now is only now
        and then

resurrected
morning pink sweeps back the stars
plows under the night and sows a path
for the sun to surge into the next and the next
breaking free of its gilded sutures to singe across
the landscape of our eyes, our skin, our hours

by light
shadows grow long in exchange
for time, so easy
to forget that one day, one last
sunset will burn down my name
when the sky calls my ghost into flight

tomorrow
or the next or the next
when my night falls, another sun comes
after standing vigil to leap into the heavens
pry apart the dark for you
to receive the day in your waiting hands

three mississippi

one mississippi
when I first became lightning
I was driving to pick up my son
the world went impossibly bright
no time to count the seconds
to wonder who would bring my child home
before the heavens came crashing

in that nanosecond of life inside light
deafened and blinded, when I guessed
I was dead, a thousand thoughts crowded
of all the things left undone—
the syrup bottle on the counter
the dog waiting next to his leash
all the words not laid inside
the soft shells of my children's ears

for hours, the smell and taste of ozone
my trembling hands
reminded me that I had been placed
back into myself by powers far beyond
my own and I was grateful
to put away the syrup
to clip leash to collar
to whisper over the sleeping cocoons of my boys

two mississippi
the second time I became lightning
my dog led me beyond the trees
the clouds had grown necrotic and eerie
dropping low as they spiraled upward
I called to Atlas and we hurried
down from the balded ridge
away from what brewed
we hadn't yet reached the low ground

when everything popped into brightness
its intensity too much to comprehend
there still wasn't time to count
before the heavens cracked open

sending Atlas crying to my feet
but this time, in front of x-rayed tree trunks
I saw a miracle
an orb where lightning stabbed
down from the sky and snaked
up from the earth, meeting mid-air
as though summoned by the branches,
conjured by the wizarding elements

the electric scent of ozone made me think
the idea of dying this way
not by storm but in a magical flash
a sudden bolt that outruns pain
and outlasts time in its fractional existence
might be the best way to leave
the waning cavern of my body

three mississippi
the last time I become lightning
I want it to be like this:
when my sons are strong and weathered
like the stones that form the ridge
when maybe most of all those undone things
have been crossed off and Atlas and all the dogs
that will come after him have gone
to hold up the heavens as they wait
for us to return to them   then
in a brilliant burst, my soul takes flight
out of time   I am released
into a billion particles of light

communion

placed
as I am here
a ghost housed
like an egg nested
deep in mangroves inside
the chaos of vessels and sinew
of bone and sponge where blood runs
at the speed of life

given
this gift of breath
I am to learn to see
other miracles that breathe
and fly and sway and tower tall
I feel the weighted pull of obligation
to feast the eyes until memory is bursting
with the color of living

brief
this time of communion
with the rattle and thrust
of seed pods pushed by new life
of indigo night cracked open by light
the wind strumming through pine needles
like a lover's fingers and this is how I know
a tree can feel love

wondering
mind wandering heart
each beat one closer to last
I could run so fast I leave myself
far behind never on time but following
if I ever catch up time will have already
caught up to me and I am back among the stars
blinking my astonishment

the shape of sound

the color orange did not exist to the english
until the fruit arrived and proved itself
but did they see it, did they wonder
how an impression that filled their eyes had no name?

blue went ignored by the greek,
chinese and hebrew and japanese
yet still the sky held its breath knowing
one day they would notice and claim

did you know that bats hear shapes carved
by sound ricocheting into ears that interpret
forms we have named for corners and curves
we measure only with our eyes?

or that bees fly home to dance maps—
can you imagine finding a flower
deep in a field among thousands of twins
because your sister stomped her feet?

think about plants eating light and trees talking
to each other by clasping hands deep inside the earth
deer fleeing for higher ground when the seething
heat beneath us mutters in a language we have forgotten

what will you find when you shed your heartfed
confines, when you drop your rules and realize
you have been breathing time all along
as you sigh and walk into the air?

salmon fly

oh
dear dragonfly
you have fallen from the sky
slender indigo spinning
where my finger breaks the current
your spent body finished
fighting the constant pull
of gravity and now sliding fast
down the creek where

the fall
salmon has the audacity
to try going against time
summer fat he lumbers
against the flow, labors to find that place
he remembers, beats himself
into red completion and loses in the end
or does he win by starting over
did he win after all?

bodies empty
blend with battered leaves
caught in the rocks filtering
the rapid pour as their shells give in
to flow and their tiny pieces break
free to sail on ever smaller until
one with the water they fly into the heat
of the afternoon's copper harvest
breathed in by the sun and

reborn as clouds

the memory   of glaciers

I won't see when I've gone   home or to bed or beyond the stars
but while I wade   through dreams or whatever happens
when we're done   the river will run
and run and run   birthed from an earth
that takes back   as quickly as it gives
a question   it never asks
will you die   as well as you lived?
because the answer   is already poured
into its slippery throat   with the memory
of glaciers and gullies   of tears shaken loose
from the clouds just as   the ghost that keeps me mortal
who finally outran me   slides creek to stream to river
in ever larger veins   designed to drain all the earth
holds and carry it   *hurry along now*
toward the pulsing shore   for the ocean to devour
then offer back   to the sky
there are times when   the river pulls me when
beside me I feel him   but not him
as real as the moon's face   steady
on the surface   of the water's night winding
just as impossible to grasp   now that he left
to the dark river   the lost sun beyond the stars.
someday   when I lean back over my life
and reach for the door   to see him again
will the maps etched in my skin   mean anything
will the compass of my bones…   my point?
the mountain tumbles   into the ocean
winter's snow yields to the tide   the light fades to the edge
of the horizon where water   can't reach
when I am delivered of my breath   I will understand then
the importance of breathing   but the river will reclaim
that space in my lungs   what I borrowed long ago
when I burst   into the light
will the water wave as I enter   *hello and goodbye you*
or will the river run and run   slickblack indifference

moonscattered with shine   that rests in silence
    on its face bright   as stars seeded
    across the night sky   waiting
    for the next one   to fall

even as

nighthawks call out
the coordinates
of the precise spot
shadow will rush
from the earth to meet
the falling night

pines sip the sun's last
needling blue into color
that sews itself deep
into starlit black leaving
behind the divine
an indigo memory

of a day spent wide
in sage kissing the air
just before quick rain
that pocked the dust
as a reminder that answers
fall from above

now, forgotten light
hidden as we traverse
the dark and slow, slow
in this moment I know
I've never put together
a proper prayer

when night comes
follow the strung stars
feel the darkness rise
speak lightly of heaven
and let the coyotes sing
sing us home

the ones who leave the ground

the shout of fall's first leaf
clashing prayer of colors
pansies hang their feline heads

                      last sun-soaked flower stretched wide
                      this is my heart bursting open

horizon lavender with snow
diminishing cricketsong
weaves a golden threaded finale

                      antiqued coin rusted sunset
                      this is the shade between my ribs

the humble bees bumble
through slender yellowed lilies
reclined along the slowing river

                      soon embalmed by winter
                      this is my blood still moving

chipper chickadee shadow hops
shakes livid branches to see what falls
fat and frantic search for seeds

                      stark kenning of roots pulling up
                      this is my spine tilting earthward

on the skyline the day buries its bones
lost in a canary stir of leaves
whispers goodbye to the fallen light

                      generous gloss of the moon
                      this is the mirror behind my eyes

sewn as the trees are to change
naked they reach for the future
let it breathe   let it breathe

                        the late sparrow takes flight
                        this is how I will leave

argentum

I see you there, silver
as you fade, brighter now
because I notice, because I know
the shadow running at us
in this shining moment
now, I understand kenning
the interpretation of my rhythms
informing me:
the gift, you see
is in knowing our hearts
will break at the same time
when you leave
when you give up
your kinblood bones
for the relief of flight
I bend
nearer the seeping still
of your threadbare heart
to cover the chill growing
across your paper skin

black bird blue

and on that day, when all your birds have flown
will you lay down a last wreath of your words strung
slack, loosened from the tether of your tongue

and as you fall under the lilac haze of the springing
of your soul will you feel pulled from you a song you didn't know
you knew, chords strummed along the still of your breastbone

and when at last you see all that you couldn't
with your eyes, will you finally recognize the color
of your generosity, the size of your kindness in petals falling

and the moment your ghost flies, leaving your stunned shell
will you know the black bird there to guide you into the blue
and do you see it now
do you see it?

Broderick Eaton grew up exploring the natural world out her back door in the foothills of the Cascades. She returned permanently to the Pacific Northwest after living in Costa Rica, Virginia, and Spain. As a student at Sweet Briar College, her writing career began when she stumbled into a life-changing introduction to poet Mary Oliver. This turned into informal poetry studies and then workshops and independent classes. After college, she fell into her first adult iteration as a high school Spanish teacher and completely forgot about writing for many years. Nearly two decades later, the muses returned and demanded an audience, and the seeds sewn in that tiny office at Sweet Briar suddenly burst into bloom.

Writing for only the last few years, Eaton strives to draw parallel the inexorable rhythm of the natural environment we inhabit and the treasures to be found if only we look around us and live in the moment, in this world full of awe.

Her work has appeared in numerous publications, including *Crosswinds Poetry Journal*, *Smartish Pace*, *Writer's Digest*, *Slippery Elm*, and *Verseweavers*. When she began sending her work out, she won first place for new poets in an Oregon Poetry Association contest, followed shortly by the Sixfold Poetry Prize. Her poems have also been named runner-up for the Erskine J. Poetry Prize, and finalist for both the 49th Parallel Award and the Tucson Festival of Books poetry award.

She has an MFA in Writing with a poetry emphasis from Lindenwood University and lives in the high desert of Oregon with her family, a dog who is a real-life Clifford, the greatest cat ever to grace humans with its presence, and a handful of chickens named for Schitt's Creek characters.

Learn more about Broderick Eaton at broderickeaton.com.

www.ingramcontent.com/pod-product-compliance
Lightning Source LLC
LaVergne TN
LVHW041505070426
835507LV00012B/1341